Virgo

THIS BOOK BELONGS TO:

_____

THE WONDERFUL WORLD OF ZODIACS

VIRGO

Mimi Jones

Dedicated to my daughter, Becca.

All rights reserved.
No part of this book may be reproduced in any form or by any means, electronic or mechanical, and no photocopying or recording, unless you have written permission from the author.

ISBN 978-1-958985-53-3

Text copyright © 2025 by Mimi Jones

www.joeysavestheday.com

A Mimi Book

Element:
Virgo is an Earth sign.

♍

VIRGO

 # Ruling Planet:

Mercury rules Virgo.

Symbol:

The Maiden represents Virgo.

 # Personality:

Virgos are known for being analytical and practical.

PERFECTIONISTIC

Weakness:

Virgos can be overly critical and perfectionistic.

virgo

Color:

Their lucky colors are green, beige, and brown.

Lucky Numbers:

5, 14, 15, and 23 are lucky for Virgos.

Compatibility:

Virgo gets along well with Taurus, Capricorn, Cancer, and Scorpio.

Dislikes:

They dislike messiness and chaos.

Virgo

Likes:

Virgos love organization, helping others, and intellectual pursuits.

Career:

They excel in careers that require precision and problem-solving.

Positive Trait:

Virgos are very hardworking and practical.

Negative Trait:

Sometimes, they can be too self-critical.

Virgo

Motto:

Their motto is "I analyze."

I
ANALYZE

Favorite Day:

Wednesday is their favorite day.

WEDNESDAY

Health:

Virgos should take care of their digestive system and intestines.

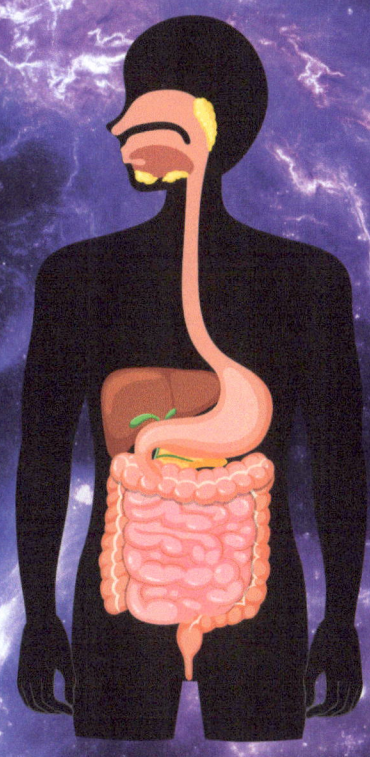

Style:

They prefer clean, elegant, and understated styles.

Challenges:
Virgos need to learn to accept imperfection and let go of unnecessary stress.

Friendship:

They are loyal friends who will always offer a helping hand.

Influence:

They inspire others with their work ethic and dedication.

VIRGO

Favorite Activities:

Virgos love activities that involve learning and improving their skills.

Symbolic Animal:

The Maiden symbolizes their purity and attention to detail.

Birthstones:

The birthstones for Virgo are peridot and sapphire.

If this Zodiac gem tickled your celestial fancy, then you're in for a treat! Dive into my other Zodiac delights right here:

www.mimibooks.com

THE END!

www.ingramcontent.com/pod-product-compliance
Lightning Source LLC
Chambersburg PA
CBHW040030050426
42453CB00002B/71